MW01225292

MUTUAL AWAKENING

OPENING INTO A NEW PARADIGM OF HUMAN RELATEDNESS

Patricia Albere and Jeff Carreira

Photography by Laria Saunders

Mutual Awakening

Opening into a New Paradigm for Human Relatedness

Copyright © 2013 Patricia Albere and Jeff Carreira

All rights reserved. Except as permitted under U.S. Copyright Act of 1976, no part of this publication may be reproduced, distributed, or transmitted in any form or by any means, or stored in a database or retrieval system, without the prior written permission of the authors.

Published by

The Evolutionary Collective

Santa Fe, NM 87509

ISBN-13: 978-0615922454

ISBN-10: 0615922457

Book Design by Free Agency

www.choosefreeagency.com

Photography by Laria Saunders

www.lariasaunders.com

Photographs of Patricia & Jeff by Doug Ciarelli

And to our friend Shelly Souza, thank you so much for your invaluable editorial support.

TABLE *of* CONTENTS

an *INVITATION* to *MUTUAL AWAKENING*

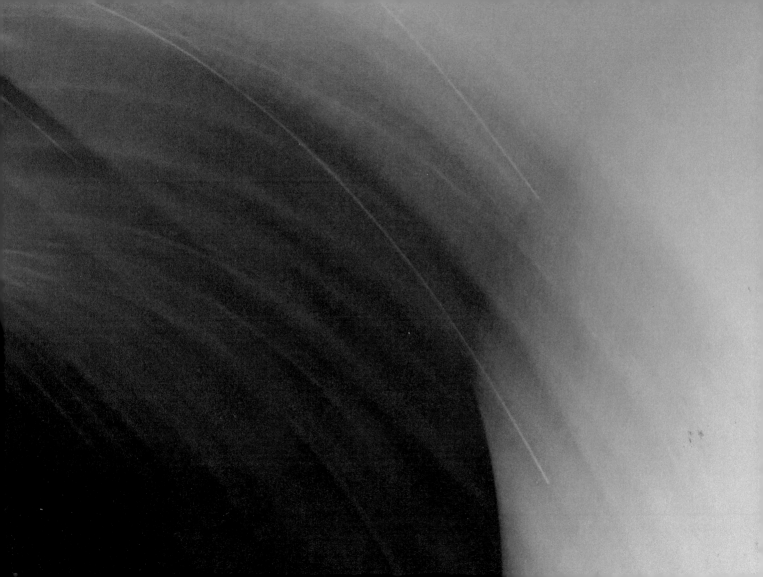

This book is an introduction to a profound spiritual practice called Mutual Awakening. In truth it is better described as a variety of practices of similar form generally worked with in pairs or small groups. These practices, when guided masterfully, lead those engaged into a shared awakening of consciousness not only within the individuals themselves but more importantly in the space between them.

Our only hesitation in releasing this book is that describing this practice outside of the context of the overall spiritual work of the Evolutionary Collective of which it is a part gives a partial picture. Certainly the practices of Mutual Awakening are powerfully transformative. At the same time they are part of a larger design of spiritual work, and they bestow their greatest blessings only within that context.

Mutual Awakening practices open us to profound experiences of shared awakened consciousness. This unification of heart, mind, and soul, and the potential inherent in it, is the real point. That is the yonder shore that is calling us. In these brief introductory words we only want to remind you that a practice is only a vehicle and encourage you to keep your attention on the destination.

Please read this book with openness and vulnerability. Allow yourself to be carried into a new world of possibility. And never forget that this is an invitation to a journey that can take you much further than any spiritual practice alone could ever do.

the BIRTH of MUTUAL AWAKENING

A Personal Narrative from Patricia Albere

Chapter 1

THE PRACTICE of Mutual Awakening leads to the living realization of awakened mutuality. The discovery and true embodiment of that possibility is what this is all about.

I am not a practitioner by nature. Although I can operate inside of structure and discipline, I've found that everything that has had held real power and beauty in my life has arisen through risk, flow, and allowing myself the intensity of direct encounter with reality. Practices and techniques pale in comparison to the heart expanding experience of real contact with the divine. At the same time I know that spiritual practices, when embraced with real intention and a pure heart, have the power to bring us into direct contact with the miraculous.

It is strange for me to think of Mutual Awakening as a "practice" because that's not how it appeared in my life. What actually happened is that I had the profound grace of entering into a relationship that opened into a mutually awakened way of being. That relationship soon ended tragically, and it was only in the years that followed that I pieced together a puzzle that lead to the practice of Mutual Awakening.

By most standards I have lead an amazing life. I was a precocious child, and as my life unfolded I have always found myself drawn to the edge of everything. I think this maverick spirit is in my DNA. My ancestors came to this continent in the early 1600s and participated in the struggle to establish a living experiment of democratic ideals. I feel deeply connected to my revolutionary ancestry, and I can only imagine that there is some inheritance there that leads me to follow the urging of the edge. Somehow, at crucial times in my life, I always seem to show up at the beginning of something big.

I went to Woodstock when I was fifteen. I had heard something about a weekend concert. No one seemed to know much about what it was, but I knew I had to be there. When I told my mother of my plans, I wasn't really asking for permission. I knew I was going. My mother seemed to intuit early in my life that the best way to handle my precociousness was to trust me and be supportive. So I arrived at Woodstock with my mother's blessing.

I graduated from high school a few years later and felt compelled to move to California and be there for a year prior to attending college. It wasn't that I knew something special about California; it was an unquestioned intuition that I followed. Once again I found myself in an epicenter I hadn't known existed. I moved into a yellow Victorian house in a district called Haight-Ashbury with no idea that I had arrived at the apex of the counterculture.

Soon after moving into our house on Haight Street, a schoolmate from high school, living in San Francisco, came to visit. She told me about a seminar she had just done called Mind Dynamics with someone named Werner Erhard. I had no idea what she was talking about. She felt different in a way that was intriguing, and I knew I had to go to his next seminar. I told my mother about it, and she mailed me the $300 for tuition, writing the check directly to Mind Dynamics so I wouldn't use it for the rent.

During that weekend seminar the world, my experience of myself, and what I saw as possible was irrevocably transformed. I had to be part of what was happening. I went to Werner and asked him for a job. For some reason he said yes. So at eighteen years old I started working for Werner Erhard four months before he would initiate the personal transformation

phenomenon known as EST and later Landmark Education.

All I wanted was to share the miracle that had opened up for me with others. Soon I was speaking seven nights a week. The audiences grew until I was addressing thousands of people in venues like New York City's Lincoln Center. Eventually I was responsible for training others to do what I was doing—awaken people to their true potential and inspire them to realize it. For the next thirteen years I played a prominent role in expanding EST's reach into the world, speaking to hundreds of thousands of people and training some of the organization's leaders.

My story was only just beginning. After I left EST I met a beautiful young German man, named Peter. He was a deeply meditative mystic, and we fell in love. As extraordinary as it was, my time at EST could not have prepared me for what I encountered with Peter. Our love was a wholehearted expression of being fully "met" in all dimensions of love—from simple, sweet human tenderness to sacred union. We were an unambivalent "yes" to each other and to the reality of love itself. The force of our encounter undid me, and I surrendered again to being transformed.

The depth of spiritual connection in our love was palpable, and we each knew we had finally met a partner who was aligned with the deepest longings of our own heart. We began to experience spiritual openings that were continuous and intense. Each next awakening revealed more beauty, love, and authenticity than either of us had encountered alone. Any patterns or habits that created separation spontaneously revealed themselves, and we relentlessly passed through them into ever-deeper union.

Divine love, if surrendered to, is incessant and insatiable in its desire for more of itself. It dissolves, shatters, and transforms anything that blocks love's path toward deeper love. The isolated sense of self that we could call the ego is a by-product of our experience of the lack of love. The ego is an endless chain of habitual activity and reactivity that we mistakenly assume will lead to love. Real love is "beingness" itself. It is the essence of existence. As Peter and I surrendered to the force of what was happening to us, a relational field awakened between us. The Mutual Awakening

REAL LOVE
is **BEINGNESS ITSELF.**

practice was born out of our ever-deepening surrender to the love that had engulfed us.

During the time that we were together we made love physically at least once and often many times a day. The deep physical intimacy and passionate love that I shared with this truly meditative man generated an ongoing intensity of presence and depth of consciousness between us. Over time we began to continuously abide in a miraculously telepathic state of awareness.

We were not practicing tantra; in fact I didn't know anything about tantric practices and wouldn't hear about them until years later. Making love was not a practice for us. We never manipulated our lovemaking. We surrendered to it and followed whatever was unfolding between us until eventually we were consistently swept away by something much greater than us whenever we made love. Like the masterful dancer who realizes the dance is dancing them, love was making love with itself through us with great delight and endless creativity.

The result of our openness, presence, engagement, interest, and commitment expanded beyond our physical intimacy into a living vortex of continuous transformation. There was an undeniable catalytic power awakening us together. It was purifying us and demanding that we continually open to something so much greater than ourselves. The way we were together seemed to unleash a power similar to what people often find with enlightened teachers.

During this time maintaining a continuous sense of connectedness was simply our way of being together. The thought of developing a "practice" out of it would never have occurred to me. The intensity of love and the desire to be as close as possible was the only thing moving us.

I remember once leaving our apartment on West Fifty-sixth Street in New York City and going to the grocery store nearby. We were putting things in our shopping cart, occasionally kissing and feeling very light and connected. We got to the checkout, and Peter's energy closed down just slightly. Our commitment was to never consent to a contraction in

the space between us, and so when we left the store I asked him what had happened. He said he had noticed an attractive woman in front of me dressed in European fashion. He said he had started to judge me because I dressed like an American. I laughed and said, "Yes . . . I do dress like an American." And immediately the space between us opened up again. The secret to true intimacy is so deceptively simple. It will always be found in paying attention to whatever comes between us.

On another occasion he was sleeping late while I had been awake buzzing around, getting things done. I finally came in to wake him with a cup of tea. As he sat up in bed, taking the tea from my hand, he said, "Where's my woman?" in a soft German accent. I thought he was joking, and I said, "I'm right here." He said it again, with more seriousness, and I couldn't figure out what he was doing. I answered, and he said it yet again, this time looking deeply into my eyes and pulling me onto the bed in a powerful embrace. He was asking for my full presence, and the intensity of his gesture melted my being. He said softly, "There you are." We kissed and fell into a deeper state of consciousness than we had ever shared before.

Now I see that what we shared was an ongoing demand for a "higher order of relatedness." I also recognize that there was an evolutionary impulse or optimizing force at work in the dynamic love and conscious creativity that was alive between us. Perhaps that is what some would call the "Holy Spirit" and others "Eros." Whatever it is called, it had the transformative power to shatter the imposed isolation of ego structures that would block its access to our union.

Peter and I were together for four years. He asked me to marry him, and two weeks later a terrible car accident left him badly brain injured. Eventually he died, leaving me in an impossible situation. I had to shoulder the tremendous grief of losing my fiancé and dearest love as well as the dual awakening that had been driving my every moment. He was gone, and yet I felt our ongoing connection. It was very confusing. I had no idea how to navigate through the shock, and no one seemed able to fully understand what I was going through or could help me in any real way.

After a period of intense grieving, I innocently concluded that because I had been capable of this level of connection once I would be able to have it again. I was driven to understand what had happened to me and recreate it in my life. I initiated a deep examination of my experience to truly discover what it was that had made that dual awakening possible. Eventually I realized that what had happened to us didn't live in the romantic level of our love—even though that was where it had arisen.

I continued my journey, teaching and learning, hungry to deepen my realization and gain a clearer understanding of all the dimensions of my experience. For nine years I studied with A. H. Almaas (Hameed Ali) in the Diamond Approach. I have often called Hameed the "Einstein of spiritual realization." His comprehensive and fully embodied brilliance in all dimensions of awakened consciousness allowed me to complete a certain level of awakening, especially in the experience of what he calls "the pearl," which is the unique dimension of the soul.

Recently it has become clear that it is only now that the full understanding and true potential of what I had experienced years ago can become widely available. Culturally we have not been ready to awaken in this level of relatedness and were not able to see it for what it is. After decades of intensive individual work, we are now ready to awaken together. In fact I am certain that there are levels of development that we can only reach through the kind of unified field of consciousness that Peter and I had been so deeply immersed in.

The dual awakening experience holds the key to the future. At this point in history we must develop the ability to turn towards the space between us in a stance of receptive surrender. When we do, we enter into a dimension of unity and connection that as human beings we know is not only the truth of our connection but what we need to live together. It activates and unleashes a profound level of spiritual creativity and care that will move humanity's consciousness to the next stage.

For years I kept asking, "How do I give people access to this powerful and catalytic dimension of consciousness?" Eventually I began to discover how to do it. I found myself able to use simple exercises that would consistently give people access to true mutuality. Gradually I came to understand how to come together and initiate the miraculous unfolding of dual awakening. This was the birth of the Mutual Awakening Practice.

The work of the Evolutionary Collective is committed to creating a new paradigm for a higher order of human relating. The opening that Peter and I had was the initiation point of this work. Our love created an access point for dual awakening, and now more of us must enter on the path of awakening together so that a new expression of divine love and creativity can move through us, as us. "It" needs us to be available so that something much bigger than us can happen. Peter and I made ourselves available for heaven to manifest on earth between us. It is time now for a much larger coming together.

from
MEDITATION
to MUTUAL
AWAKENING

Chapter 2

I AM a mystic by inclination. And as a mystic I am most interested in making direct contact with the miraculous. But I am also a spiritual practitioner, and I know from twenty years of engagement with meditation that practices, when surrendered to sincerely, lead to the direct encounter of what we seek.

When Patricia Albere introduced me to the Mutual Awakening practice I approached it as any true practitioner would, with respect and passion. I soon began to have breakthrough experiences that opened new realms of realization to explore. These realizations were different from what I had experienced in meditation. At the same time the capacity to open into them was dependent on the same willingness to give up control that had opened me to the miracles of meditation.

In the next few pages I will illuminate the power of this practice by re-counting my own journey into it.

A few days before Patricia and I were to make our public teaching debut we met for a planning session at her small but beautiful apartment on the Upper East Side of New York City. We had been working together by phone for months, but this was going to be the first in-person meet-ing since our partnership began. I walked in wearing dress shoes and a button-down shirt. She was barefoot wearing faded blue jeans torn at the knees. It all seemed perfect.

In the days just prior to our planning session there had been one thing bothering me, and when I saw her I blurted it out almost immediately.

"One thing you need to know," I said. "I don't do eye-gazing."

"Why not?" she asked.

I didn't have an answer. In searching my thoughts I found no truly solid reason, just a strong conviction that I didn't feel comfortable with it because in my mind it was associated with overly sentimental, "feel good" spiritual practices. Of course I'd never done any eye-gazing, nor seen anyone do it, so I didn't have any actual experience on which to base my conviction.

"I don't do eye-gazing either," she said with a smile, and then she instructed, "Sit down; this won't hurt you."

We sat down and looked into each other's eyes for about five minutes. She was right. It didn't hurt. In fact I quickly forgot all about what we were doing and fell into a very sweet and powerful meditative state, and a deep sense of connection began to emerge between us.

It was only a few minutes, but even in that time I could feel that in our encounter something was pulling. It wasn't personal attraction, or sentimentality. It was a call into depth and sacredness. By letting my prejudices drop for a few minutes I found myself being pulled toward a space between us that felt profound and limitless.

Patricia and I have been teaching together continuously ever since that first meeting, and we still don't do eye-gazing. But we do experiment with lots of paired spiritual work that we call Mutual Awakening practice.

In these paired practices you often sit face to face with a partner, ideally one who shares your commitment to mystical revelation. Together you and your partner focus on a single or a series of simple guiding questions, answering them repeatedly for a few minutes. If you find the courage to let go, you enter into a state of spontaneous sharing in which your words seem to leap out of your mouth from a place deep inside your soul.

I believe that Mutual Awakening occurs in the meeting of one soul with another. By "soul" I simply mean the deepest place in your being, the essence of who you are. What happens in these beautiful encounters is both overwhelming and illuminating at the very same instant.

During one recent intensive weekend I was engaging in profound encounters of this type in a room full of people who were having similar encounters all around me. The energy in the room was tremendous and seemed to be building without limit. At one point I had the opportunity to do the practice with Patricia and quickly found myself in a mystical vision of a yet-to-be-manifest future possibility.

As she and I sat facing each other giving voice to our experience of the moment, I became enraptured in a vision of a world made of liquid light. In this world of light golden ribbons of stardust seemed to be falling continuously from invisible heavens. The light was bathing everyone in luminosity, or rather we appeared as beings of pure luminous form. I was held in rapture for a few precious minutes witnessing this world formed

ONE SOUL MEETS ANOTHER

of liquid light.

I had no thoughts about it, but afterward I realized that I had been gifted with a poetic image of a new world, not as it already exists but as a future possibility that has not yet been manifest.

Once I experienced how sitting face-to-face could open up portals to profound spiritual revelation I immediately saw parallels to my individual meditation practice. These two practices and the depths they open are different but related. The connection between them, as I said earlier, is that both rely on our willingness to give up control of our experience and allow revelation to overtake our hearts and minds.

In meditation, while sitting silently on a cushion, I strive to simply allow whatever is present to be there. My goal in meditation is to be with reality exactly the way it is without manipulating or controlling it in any way. As I sit, I keep letting go of all of the subtle habits of manipulation and control, and I drift ever closer to perfect union with what is. The ultimate consciousness of deep meditation is one of absolute unity—a oneness in which we disappear. If you are fortunate enough to experience even a moment so deep, you discover the liberating truth of who you were before you were born—prior to your existence here in this body, living this life, in this world.

Practicing meditation in this way is like removing your hands from the steering wheel and your foot from the gas pedal while driving down the freeway. If you are successful in letting go, you discover the way things are when you are not controlling and manipulating. You discover the truth. And in this discovery at a very a deep level you have the opportunity to give yourself over to mysterious spiritual energies that initiate a process of awakening within you.

Two decades ago I stepped out of a fairly traditional life and reassembled myself around a spiritual commitment to a community and a teacher. For twenty years I devoted myself more or less exclusively to spiritual attainment with very little distraction. My energy during all those years was devoted to my own ever-deepening awakening and my efforts to mentor and teach others in support of their awakening. In the space of this chapter I cannot begin to share the full extent of the spiritual experiences I was blessed with during that time. One of the foundations of my spiritual practice was meditation, and through that practice I experienced energetic openings and spiritual breakthroughs beyond my wildest dreams.

I have experienced the sacred grace of having any sense of limitation fall away. In this experience of spiritual liberation it is as if you had been wearing a lead suit all of your life. It is a mental straight jacket made up of all your ideas about what is possible and what is not. In the instant of liberation it simply drops away. Suddenly you find yourself blissfully free of constraining beliefs, not knowing what is ultimately possible, and compelled by the call of a wide-open future.

During long retreats I have had the opportunity to spend days, weeks, and even months absorbed in meditative unfolding. Many of the awakenings I experienced had the power to dislodge the source of my awareness from its habitual attachment to the mind and body. I have abided for days in states of constant consciousness through periods of both wakefulness and sleep; experienced the energy of Kundalini coursing through my body with white light pouring through the top of my head; and had the grace of merging with others in shared states of collective higher mind that animated all of us.

These experiences and many more have left me certain that reality will always be bigger than I can imagine. I know that we are not ultimately restricted by the limitations of the mind and body, and as long as we continue to surrender the openings and awakenings will go on forever. There is no end to the mysteries of the inner life.

As with meditation, the goal in Mutual Awakening is to be with reality exactly as it is, except this practice is done with another in a spontaneous and immediate flow of shared experience rather than an individual experience. As you look at your partner and repeatedly answer the simple guiding question over and over, it can initially feel artificial and forced. At this stage of the practice you are still drawing mainly on your intellect.

If you continue to let go, you will begin to find that you forget the person in front of you, and you forget yourself. Your attention is drawn to something that is emerging between you. What arises is not appearing outside of you, and yet it is not arising inside of you exclusively. As your experience of the practice grows, you begin to attune to the shared space between you and your partner.

As you continue to let go, words emerge from your mouth more and more spontaneously. They seem to be describing your experience as quickly as you are having it. The intellect is no longer the source of what you are saying. The words emerge from a deeper source of your being, and you realize that you are saying things you never could have imagined before.

Often in Mutual Awakening practice what emerges is poetry. I have found that if I follow the words as they emerge and avoid the temptation to adorn them with meaning, I can follow the trail of spontaneous utterances into

new worlds of possibility.

When you go deeply enough into the practice of meditation, you eventually realize that there is no end. You can follow that practice forever into deeper revelations. The same is true of Mutual Awakening practice. It never ends. You and your partner move into ever-deeper openings and realizations. And because you are together the space you are exploring is inherently relational. You do experience a kind of oneness, but it is a oneness that includes you both. You find a oneness that holds relatedness.

Teaching with Patricia Albere in the Evolutionary Collective has opened another source of awakening in my life, and this is why I am so compelled by our working partnership.

I believe in all sincerity that what we need right now is real evolutionary partnerships. We have all grown tremendously through work that we have done on ourselves. We have realized so much. And now we can only go to the next level by coming together in everything that we have realized.

The next opportunity for a major leap in development will be found in a level of mutuality that we can only achieve together. When we express our deepest nature with others who are doing the same, we create a new way of being human.

As teachers, Patricia and I are committed to cultivating an emergence of this level of spiritual solidarity. I am aware how rare it is to find teachers who truly want to work mutually, especially if they have been trained in different schools and lineages. I have worked with other teachers in parallel—sharing a platform but doing our own thing. Patricia and I share a commitment to pioneer the possibility of coming together in a mutual surrender that becomes the source of what we teach. The teaching that we do in the Evolutionary Collective emerges between us, not from us.

Working with Patricia and the other extraordinary people in the Evolutionary Collective has initiated a new opening in me and given me a new understanding of what is possible for all of us. I am honored to have the opportunity of this book to share this opening with you.

MYSTICISM & MUTUAL AWAKENING

Chapter 3

MYSTICISM IS the realm of human
endeavor aimed at making direct contact with divine spiritual truths that are generally hidden from view. It has long been the bastion of men and women who could not be satisfied with the world as it is. These spiritual adventurers acquired an appetite for the miraculous that could only be satiated by authentic divinity. For thousands of years men and women of different spiritual traditions have followed mystical paths into the higher reaches of human potential. Those who had the courage and commitment to embody what they found there became harbingers of new ways of being human.

When we engage in the practice of Mutual Awakening, we see potentials for human relatedness that carry us beyond separation. These experiences often come to us as mystical visions and intuitions, which point toward heights of connection that capture our imagination and ignite our hearts. The core work of the Evolutionary Collective shares many qualities often associated with traditional mystical paths, and in this chapter we will explore some of these and add some that are more specific to the particular mysticism of Mutual Awakening.

Mystics gaze into the deeper reality that lies hidden beneath our ordinary experience. They know that what we see on the surface, and much of what we have been told is true, is a very shallow view of what exists. Mystics see beyond consensus reality into a never-ending depth. Once they taste the mystical realm their hearts are blown open, and the flow of divine love overtakes them, and they cannot return to anything less.

The mystic travels beyond the ordinary, and because their destination is beyond what is known, they are forced to travel with nothing but the light of a passionate heart to guide them. Like the mystic, those of us who awaken to a new possibility for human relatedness must follow our heart's longing and travel into unknown realms beyond our ordinary experience.

Many of us sense that there is a possibility for human relatedness that could radically change life as we know it. We have had moments when we have seen that possibility. Often it is triggered by a gesture of extraordinary honesty, intimacy, or kindness. In those moments we have a glimpse of how glorious human relatedness can be. The level of relationship that we normally experience pales in comparison. These moments are revelations of a higher order of human relatedness, and Mutual Awakening practice invites these glimpses and then expands and ultimately stabilizes them in our experience.

What is the possibility of human relatedness that is compelling you to read this book?

You probably have a sense of what has inspired you to this point. You know that a possibility of relatedness exists that is sacred, authentic, and demanding in the most splendid ways imaginable. You have tasted it even though it does not yet fully exist. You can point out examples of what it is not. You might also be able to give some account of what qualities such a relationship would have. At the same time you find it difficult to capture entirely in words. You feel the possibility of this relatedness in your heart, but you struggle to describe or explain it. The challenge of capturing these experiences in words is one of the qualities that our intuitions of higher relatedness share with all traditional mystical experiences. In fact, there are three characteristics traditionally associated with mystical experiences that we will recognize in our own intuitions of higher relatedness.

The first quality of mystical experiences is that they defy ordinary description or explanation. Those of us who have them find ourselves at a loss to effectively share them with others. The second is that such experiences, while frustrating our efforts to explain them, also contain an undeniable intuitive wisdom. Those who are blessed with them experience their profound meaning and significance even if we are unable to explain them fully. The last quality that clearly marks these experiences as mystical in nature is that they are transitory and often fleeting in nature. They arrive unexpectedly and depart in their own time. They cannot be controlled, and no amount of will power will ever tame them.

The great mystics through the ages have all discovered that mystical experiences cannot be approached as means to other ends. If we treat them as such they will remain beyond our grasp. Our awakening is not in service of our agendas. The experiences we awaken to are in service of a new possibility for all of humanity. The true mystic knows this. They do not pursue the miraculous in order to discover something that they will use for themselves. They only want to experience that possibility directly. The mystic is in love—in love with what can be. And the path of mysticism is one of surrender and embrace of the ultimate emerging possibility.

If we want to fulfill our spiritual longings, we must come to terms with the nature and demands of the mystical path. The deeper doorways that

a NEW POSSIBILITY for HUMANITY

can open in the practice of Mutual Awakening will remain closed as long as our motivation is primarily one of personal gain. To the degree that we are attempting to use this practice to gain insight and understanding that we believe will benefit us later, we will not be fully available; we will be holding back, saving ourselves for that time when we imagine we will use our experience to improve our lives. We will not be able to fully give ourselves to where the practice wants to take us until we are ready to let go. Until then the deeper mysteries will remain hidden.

The mystical revelation of a new possibility of relatedness is available as soon as we truly want it. That is the miracle. It is here already, waiting for us to want it on its terms. Many find this challenging to live up to. We want the miraculous, but we want to control its manifestation. What is illuminated in these realizations is too large to control.

Great saints and sages of every tradition have recognized their deepest spiritual revelations to be heralds of divine love. In profound moments of awakening we encounter the possibility of true connection with all of life and the promise of ultimate fulfillment. Revelation has its own agenda. It wants to rid us of the selfish constraints that displace the bounty of divine love. The sacred works mysteriously, in the way it wants, in its own time, not necessarily in the way we think it should to fit our timeframe. Before it will bestow its gifts, it waits until we are ready to allow them to unfold according to their own nature and not ours.

In earlier times when many great mystical traditions formed, the world was more brutal and chaotic. Mystics who longed to devote themselves to the divine felt the necessity to separate from the world and isolate themselves. They removed their attention from external reality so they could focus on the mysteries that lie within. But the world we live in today is more accommodating. We are not always forced to retreat from it in order to find solace of mind. The possibility of pursuing mystical depth in relationship is open like never before. In fact there are many today who are ready to embark on a path of higher relatedness.

The mysticism of Mutual Awakening is not a solo journey. It is an awakening that happens between people. The practice of Mutual Awakening involves putting our attention on an inner space that exists between us. It's an inner space of relatedness, and when we give ourselves to this space and follow what emerges, we experience a simultaneous sense of being completely withdrawn from the ordinary world yet completely together in a world of mystical unfolding.

In the practice of Mutual Awakening we enter into a different mystical world, and new capacities in consciousness are born in the space between us. In this new paradigm of mystical experience "we" are transformed, and the field of relatedness we share bursts to new life. In this mutual transfiguration, new possibilities in relationship appear that were not there before. It isn't relationship as we have known it. We find ourselves profoundly free of limiting ideas and cultural roles. We can do things now, say things now, and perceive things now—together—that simply were not possible before. New possibilities of love, creativity, and intelligence emerge. And as we surrender more and more to what is happening between us, our surrender opens us to ever-new possibilities of relatedness. In the Evolutionary Collective we call this new possibility we-mysticism, and it is a spiritual journey that can only be accomplished with at least one other.

The shared awakening of we-mysticism occurs when we come together not knowing who we are, who the other is, or what is possible between us. In this profoundly open and receptive state we engage together and allow an unfolding to begin. We have removed our attention from the familiar and entered into a state of mutually generated revelation. This revelation occurs in the inner space between us and can only be entered mutually.

The revelations of we-mysticism have two characteristics that differentiate them from more traditional forms of mysticism. These features are collective transparency and spiritual interdependency.

Initially when individuals come together they are opaque to each other. We see the outer surface of the other, but the inner workings of mind, heart, and soul remain hidden from view. In the we-mystical experience we enter into a state of collective transparency, and the surfaces that separate us fall away. We begin to see into and through each other. As the sense of separation falls away, we simultaneously become more aware of ourselves, more aware of the other and newly aware of a collective being that is independent from us and created by us at the same time.

The heights of awareness that open up in the we-mystical state are only revealed between individuals. The mutual nature of this experience awakens us to a shared sense of responsibility for the sacred consciousness we now hold in common. We realize that access to these deeper places in each other and the beautiful space of relatedness that is unfolding are being held between us. In this realization we feel a sense of sacred obligation and vulnerability. In this spiritual interdependency we are both responsible for the sacred portal that has opened up and reliant on each other to maintain it.

Earlier we said that mystical experiences defy description, but that isn't entirely true. Great saints and sages have communicated the profound

wisdom inherent in mystical states for millennia. Often this transmission is accomplished though the mere presence of a realizer. So deeply connected is he or she to the source of truth that merely by being in their close proximity we are lifted into the same state of being in which they abide.

It is also true that words can carry mystical transmission. Poets have long known that words can be used to move us beyond literal meaning into shared experiences of the ineffable that lie beyond all words. Great poets throughout the ages have used words to communicate profound emotion, sacred insight, and mystical vision. The poem takes language beyond the limits of literal communication and becomes an instrument of attunement that brings our awareness into direct contact with the experience the poet wants to share.

In Mutual Awakening practice language similarly becomes an instrument of conscious attunement that carries us into mutually shared revelations of new possibilities. This practice invites us to use language with a degree of flexibility and fluidity that allows our words to formulate spontaneously in direct response to experience as it arises. We let a poetic spirit overtake us. Our language becomes more imaginative, metaphorical, and beautiful as it unfolds. A space of limitless possibility opens up that allows the mystery of the unknown to come through us so that we move beyond the ordinary into the extraordinary.

We-mysticism demands a form of language that invites novelty. In the Evolutionary Collective we call this use of language Improvisational Transformative Poetics.

Our use of language is improvisational because it proceeds without preconception. We don't know what we are going to say ahead of time. In Mutual Awakening practice we do not speak about our experience; we give our experience a voice. We are not looking at our experience and describing it. We are allowing that experience to take us over and speak through us so that even we are amazed at what comes out of our mouths. When this direct communication happens, a spontaneous process of divine discourse unfolds.

Our use of language is transformative when its aim is not to inform but to transform. Words have the power to change us, and in we-mysticism that power is harnessed to fuel profound spiritual awakening. When we allow our sublime experiences to have a voice, we speak with a sacred authority and authenticity. We enter into a communion in which our shared intention is to open ourselves to the full creative potential of relatedness. We serve this transformative function by surrendering our voice and giving it over to the vision and wisdom that is emerging between us.

Our use of language is poetic because it is aimed at that which lies beyond what words can express. We are giving voice to a level of consciousness that abides beyond what the mind can know and cannot be captured in ordinary terms. And so in this practice we give ourselves poetic license to be inventive with words, to allow meaning to spontaneously generate through us, anchored only in the truth that moves us, free from references to the past. Our words, liberated through the surrender of a mystical heart, are fueled by inspiration, not by understanding.

Improvisational Transformative Poetics is a fluid and free use of language that gives the Mutual Awakening practice the power to evoke the unexpected and the miraculous. It is one of the core practices of the Evolutionary Collective, and it does have the power to bring us into direct contact with a new world of relatedness.

a NEW PARADIGM of HUMAN RELATEDNESS

Chapter 4

IT IS A FACT of human history that para-
digm shifts do occur—new worlds do open up—and whenever they do it is because some group of individuals found the courage to leave one paradigm behind and embrace a new one. It is nothing less than a shift from one reality to another. It is a journey into a new world. Those who are first to venture forward on this journey must do so without agreement from the majority because they are seeing a possibility that others do not yet see.

We all see the world through a preexisting paradigm or worldview that acts as a filter, allowing us to perceive only in ways that align with what we already believe to be true. In other words, we see the world through a set of beliefs about the world, and these beliefs shape our experience of reality. When a paradigm shift occurs, the world changes shape. Our experience of reality alters. We are on the same planet, but the world is different. We are in a new reality. As with any true spiritual practice, the Mutual Awakening practice is a doorway into a different reality—a new world. It has often been the mystics of any age that have played the role of harbingers of new paradigms because they have ventured into possibilities far beyond the norms of their time.

The work of the Evolutionary Collective is an experiment in unleashed creativity and divine love. Our aim is to co-create a new world and shift into a new paradigm of human relatedness. Mutual Awakening practice opens doorways of experience that reveal this new world of possibility. It is a world that initially shows itself indistinctly in the form of intuitions, images, and sensations. If we continue the practice, deeper insights and realizations gradually begin to give this new possibility shape and form. As the shapes and forms become clear, we have the opportunity to learn to embody them in our lives. The embodiment of new possibilities is the perfect description of the work of the Evolutionary Collective, and it is exactly how paradigms shift and new worlds are born.

The most vivid historical example of a paradigm shift is the cultural change that took place during the European Enlightenment of the seventeenth and eighteenth centuries. During the span of two centuries, the dominant perception of reality shifted from the God-centered world of the medieval church to a world of scientific thought, rationality, and experimentation. A new world was born.

In the eighteenth and nineteenth centuries certain artists and intellectuals known as the Romantics began to cast a critical eye toward the advances of the Age of Reason. This literary and cultural movement introduced the initial stirrings of another paradigm shift that many agree is yet to be fully realized. In many ways, the work of the Evolutionary Collective can be seen as an extension of the romantic imperative.

The Age of Enlightenment brought about a universe that was seen as fundamentally rational, a world governed by natural laws that could be understood, manipulated, and controlled. The Romantics saw a universe that was organic and mysterious. They embraced the rationality of the Enlightenment and at the same time felt that any belief that the universe could be controlled was naive. To them the universe would always remain infinite, mysterious, and ultimately unknowable.

The consciousness of the Enlightenment taught us to see the world as a collection of "things in space." In this view the universe is an expanse of vacuous nothingness, an empty three-dimensional stage in which inanimate things and intelligent actors exist. Part of our inheritance from this time is that we experience reality as a collection of objects that can be manipulated and controlled, and we ourselves are one of those objects.

When we are engaged in the habit of objectification, we relate to each other as things to be manipulated. At this level of relating, what we are actually connecting to is our ideas about each other. We see the other as a set of characteristics and, consciously or unconsciously, pressure them to act in accordance with how we imagine them to be.

We have all felt this pressure. Imagine a time when you were visiting old friends or family who did not see you as you are, but as they imagined you to be from some time in your past. The feeling of being objectified is the feeling of not being seen. It is stifling and limiting, and we are often disappointed to find that we act like the person they think we are, rather than who we actually are.

To enter into the new paradigm of human relatedness we must break the habit of objectification. We must move beyond seeing each other exclusively as things and make direct contact with the true immensity, complexity, and infinity of who we really are.

In this new world we recognize a continuity of being that many of the Romantics wrote about. In this we discover that we are not isolated individuals in relationships with other individuals who are separate from us. We exist within what would better be described as a field of relatedness in which we are embedded within an interpenetration of systems—self-systems, cultural systems, and belief systems.

Have you noticed that we act differently, feel differently, and think differently around some people than we do around others? Take a minute to imagine one of the places where you spend a great deal of your time—maybe at work or school. Think about the conversations you have, the thoughts you have, the way you feel in that place. Would you have the same conversations, the same thoughts, and the same feelings at the beach or spending a day with your lover in the park? This simple observation is more profound than it first appears.

Our actions, thoughts, and feelings depend on the circumstances around us. We are not separate from those circumstances. We are not isolated individuals that exist in an environment that we shape through the use of force and control. We are a dynamic part of a complex natural system, and that system includes other human beings and the interactions and connections we share. The systems we exist within shape us as much as we shape them.

As the reality of the field of relatedness opens in our experience, we find ourselves floating in a constantly shifting sea of interpenetrating systems, and we begin to see that the potential of the field can be optimized. In the Evolutionary Collective we aspire to operate in this new experience of reality by optimizing the power of the field of relatedness between us.

a CONTAINER for EVOLUTIONARY RELATIONSHIP

Chapter 5

AN EVOLUTIONARY rela-

tionship is one that leads to the continuous realization of the highest potentials of both partners. The Evolutionary Collective is a container for evolutionary relationship in which we come together in a shared commitment to explore how to engage together in ways that consistently manifest our highest potentials. We move beyond the habit of trying to control and manipulate the people around us and learn to create a collective field of spiraling upward influence.

In order to build a higher field of relatedness, the individual relationships within that field must be of a higher order—we have to start with a new way of being together, person to person.

In the Mutual Awakening practice we turn towards each other while letting go of any limiting ideas about the other or ourselves. To deepen in this practice we have to find a way to not know who they are, or who we are, so that together we can discover each other anew in every moment.

When two people enter into this relationship together, they discover both the profound particularity and uniqueness of each other while at the same time discovering the same sacred source of being at their core. Two dynamic centers, two souls, intermingle and make contact in this encounter, simultaneously discovering each other and forgetting each other, as we encounter something greater together.

In this experience we awaken to the true boundless creative possibility that exists in every moment of relatedness. Each instant of relatedness is a possibility to rediscover each other free from limiting ideas. This connection becomes a source of sacred energy, liberating insight, and divine love. And the potential of a life filled with such relationships overwhelms our imagination.

Here is one practitioner's description of her experience of Mutual Awakening:

The moment-by-moment newness of the mutual awakening process captured my heart. Each partner exchange was a merging in full nakedness with the always changing NOW. I watched the peeling of each layer/veil as they showed up and melted into the ever-present vastness in the light of awareness. My partner's sharing was a reflection of my own experience. We became one. The mind broke free from motive, agenda and influence. Vastness, Peace, Love and Joy were present.

The new world that we awaken to in Mutual Awakening practice is a world of interpenetrating existence. It is a world in which we recognize that we are fundamentally connected at the deepest source of our being.

And we discover that the wisdom and illumination that emerges through our connection is the best guidance for human life.

We have all experienced moments of authentic encounter. Moments when the veil of separation falls away and the source of our being makes direct contact with the source of another.

Can you recall a moment like this? Can you remember meeting someone so deeply that it opened you to the possibility of a new world of relatedness?

Mutual Awakening is a practice of mutually entering into authentic encounter. In these encounters we make an exhilarating connection with another and experience real relatedness.

Here is another practitioner's description of Mutual Awakening:

In the Mutual Awakening practice I gave voice to my experience, and the space in between us became enlivened like a vortex of consciousness that had a momentum of its own. It was very compelling because it was altering my sense of self, from feeling limited by my body to being draw into a vortex of consciousness in which my partner and I found ourselves united in consciousness. I realized that the experience was totally dependent on my trust in the listening of my partner. Their presence as a listener was very palpable and allowed me to let go in my expression. I kept thinking, "Wow! How can I make it richer? It's not enough. It's not enough. I want to make it richer. I want to explore it more. I want to be more grounded in this.

In the Evolutionary Collective we are creating a field of relatedness that is spiritually alive, authentically co-creative, searing with honesty, and brimming with sensitivity and care. Upon the foundation of this beautiful field of relatedness we have the opportunity to create the world anew. Together we continually awaken to higher possibilities through authentic encounter with each other and enter into a world beyond objectification.

The connections that are made in Mutual Awakening practice are part of this collective evolutionary process. They are the creative unions that become the foundation for a new way of being human.

about
PATRICIA
ALBERE

& JEFF CARREIRA

Patricia Albere is an internationally recognized contemporary spiritual teacher who has taught continuously for over forty years. Her capacity to facilitate growth through collective fields of consciousness has been developed through her work with over 150,000 people around the world. She is the founder of the Evolutionary Collective, a new model for mutual awakening. Her vision is to create an ever-expanding global community that participates in creating a new paradigm for a higher order of human relatedness. She is the host of the popular global webcast Evolutionary Collective Conversations and is completing work on a new book called WEvolution: Unleashing the Transformative Power of Relating.

Jeff Carreira embarked on a life devoted to awakening in 1992 when he met spiritual teacher Andrew Cohen and embraced the perspective of Evolutionary Enlightenment. A series of life-changing experiences led Carreira to become a prominent member of a global spiritual move-ment called EnlightenNext, where he created educational programs that supported the ongoing spiritual growth of thousands of people around the world. As a spiritual mentor and guide, he has led many people to the discovery of deeper spiritual fulfillment, and he has trained over one hundred people to share the fruits of their own awakening with others. He is also the author of two books, The Miracle of Meditation and Philosophy Is Not a Luxury.

In their collaborative work as co-leaders of The Evolutionary Collective, Albere and Carreira are exploring the transformative possibilities of a higher order of human relatedness. Together they support the growth and development of an international community of people who are committed to living on the emerging edge of spirits unfolding. They have garnered a global reputation as a potent teaching team, and their mutual passion for collective development is creating an ongoing opportunity for people to realize their highest potential in a truly co-emergent environment.

17761247R00045

Made in the USA
San Bernardino, CA
17 December 2014